Who Was
Andy Warhol?

Who Was
Andy Warhol?

by Kirsten Anderson
illustrated by Gregory Copeland

Grosset & Dunlap
An Imprint of Penguin Random House

To Meg Belviso, who reads everything I write—KA

To my rep, Deborah Wolfe, for all that she has done for me
over the years—GC

GROSSET & DUNLAP
Penguin Young Readers Group
An Imprint of Penguin Random House LLC

Text copyright © 2014 by Kirsten Anderson. Illustrations copyright © 2014 by
Penguin Random House LLC. All rights reserved. Published by Grosset & Dunlap, an
imprint of Penguin Random House LLC, 345 Hudson Street, New York, New York 10014.
The WHO HQ™ colophon and GROSSET & DUNLAP are trademarks of
Penguin Random House LLC. Printed in the USA.

Library of Congress Control Number: 2014958188

ISBN 9780448482422   10 9 8 7 6 5 4 3 2

Contents

Who Was
Andy Warhol?

In July 1962, a new art exhibit opened at
the Ferus Gallery in Los Angeles. When people
walked into the gallery, they saw thirty-two
paintings lined up on a shelf. They were paintings
of cans of Campbell's soup. Each painting showed
a different flavor of soup.

Most people thought the paintings were silly.
Critics didn't think the paintings should even
be considered art. An art gallery down the street
from the Ferus put real cans of Campbell's soup
in their window with a sign that said: DO NOT BE
MISLED. GET THE ORIGINAL. OUR LOW PRICE—
TWO FOR 33 CENTS.

Andy Warhol, the artist who painted the soup
cans, heard all the jokes. He didn't care. He liked

that people were talking about his work. He even posed for photographs in a grocery store with a shopping cart filled with Campbell's soup.

He knew his soup can paintings were a different form of art. The 1960s were an exciting time. Why not make art that was fun? Why not paint pictures that celebrated the things that people saw in everyday life?

Very few people were interested in buying the soup can paintings in 1962. But in 1996, almost thirty-five years later, the Museum of Modern Art paid $15 million for thirty-two of them. By then Andy Warhol had become one of the most important artists of the twentieth century. He had changed the way people thought about art. He had created thousands of paintings. He had made movies. He had managed a rock band. People spent time at his studio just so they could seem cool.

Andy said, "In the future, everybody will be world-famous for fifteen minutes" long before the Internet even existed and people could post videos of themselves on YouTube for the world to see. And if there was one thing Andy understood, it was how to be famous. After all, he had turned Andrew Warhola, a poor, shy boy from Pittsburgh, into Andy Warhol: art superstar and international celebrity.

Chapter 1
Pittsburgh

Andrew Warhola was born on August 6, 1928, in Pittsburgh, Pennsylvania. He had two older brothers, Paul and John. His parents, Andrej and Julia, had come to Pittsburgh from Miková,

a small village in what is now Slovakia. Andrej came to the United States in 1912. Julia wasn't able to join him until 1921. Julia was very serious about her faith, which she shared with her sons. The family belonged to the Byzantine Catholic Church.

Pittsburgh was a busy city full of factories. It was the home of many large companies, such as U.S. Steel, H. J. Heinz, and Westinghouse Electric.

Most neighborhoods were filled with the hardworking people who kept the factories going. The rich owners of the factories lived in mansions on the edges of the city.

Andrej worked in construction. Julia earned extra money by making flowers out of tin cans that she sold in wealthier Pittsburgh neighborhoods. Sometimes she worked as a house cleaner.

Andy started kindergarten when he was four. On the first day of school, a girl in his class hit him. Andy refused to go back and didn't return to school for a year. His brothers thought their mother was spoiling him.

His mother worried about Andy all the time. She let him stay home from school for the slightest reason. But when he was eight, Andy became ill with a serious disease called rheumatic fever. Andy missed two months of school that year. He spent

his days reading comic books and movie-star magazines. Andy adored movies. He once wrote a fan letter to his favorite movie star, Shirley Temple, and got back an autographed picture from her. He kept the picture for the rest of his life.

It was clear early on that Andy had a gift for art, and Julia encouraged him to draw. The nearby Carnegie Institute offered free art classes to children who showed a talent for art. Andy was selected for the classes when he was nine years old.

Andy was shy and quiet. As he grew older, the skin on his face looked ashy and pale. Doctors did not know what caused the problem. Later, he developed rosacea, a condition that made his nose turn lumpy and red. Andy hated his appearance.

He looked nothing like the glamorous movie stars he admired so much.

When Andy was just thirteen, his father died. Andrej had always thought Andy had a talent for art. He left money to help send Andy to college.

Chapter 2
Art School

In September 1945, Andy began college in the Department of Painting and Design at the Carnegie Institute of Technology (now Carnegie Mellon University). He struggled during his first year. He was only seventeen and did not have the reading or writing skills he needed for college-level work.

In college, Andy discovered something important about himself. Being shy and quiet seemed to make others want to help him. He attracted people by not saying much. When he was quiet, people wondered what he was thinking. They became interested in him. He was able to get his new classmates to help him with his schoolwork. Writing was especially difficult for Andy. He sometimes asked his friends to help write papers for him.

Even art classes weren't easy for Andy. Everyone could see that he had talent, but he never seemed to do what his teachers wanted or expected. Once, he cut one of his pictures into four pieces and handed the pieces in for four assignments. The

teachers didn't know what to do. They looked at his drawings and liked what they saw. But he hadn't done the assignment properly.

It wouldn't be right to give him a good grade.

Andy's grades were so bad at the end of his first year that he almost wasn't allowed to return to the Carnegie Institute. He begged for a second chance. He took summer-school classes and worked very hard. By the end of the summer he was allowed to resume his studies.

ANDREW CARNEGIE

THE CARNEGIE MUSEUM AND CARNEGIE MELLON UNIVERSITY IN PITTSBURGH, PENNSYLVANIA, ARE BOTH NAMED AFTER ANDREW CARNEGIE. BORN IN SCOTLAND IN 1835, ANDREW MOVED WITH HIS FAMILY TO THE PITTSBURGH AREA IN 1848. AT AGE THIRTEEN, ANDREW TOOK A LOW-PAYING JOB IN A COTTON FACTORY. HE LOVED TO READ, AND GOT MOST OF HIS EDUCATION FROM THE BOOKS AT A LIBRARY OWNED BY A LOCAL WEALTHY MAN WHO ALLOWED YOUNG WORKERS TO USE IT FOR FREE.

BY 1873, CARNEGIE STARTED HIS OWN STEELMAKING COMPANY. IN 1901, HE SOLD HIS BUSINESS FOR MORE THAN $400 MILLION. THAT'S ABOUT $11 BILLION IN TODAY'S MONEY. CARNEGIE BEGAN TO GIVE HIS MONEY AWAY. HE PAID FOR 2,509 FREE LIBRARIES IN NORTH AMERICA, THE UNITED KINGDOM, AUSTRALIA, AND NEW ZEALAND. HE GAVE MONEY TO SCHOOLS,

HOSPITALS, AND SCIENCE BUILDINGS. HE BUILT
MUSEUMS, ART AND MUSIC BUILDINGS, AND
CHURCHES IN PITTSBURGH.

CARNEGIE WAS A TOUGH BUSINESSMAN, BUT
HIS GENEROSITY HELPED MANY PEOPLE. BY THE
TIME OF HIS DEATH IN 1919, HE HAD GIVEN AWAY
$350 MILLION. THE CARNEGIE FOUNDATION IS
STILL ACTIVE TODAY, SUPPORTING EDUCATION
AND PEACE PROGRAMS.

CARNEGIE INSTITUTE OF TECHNOLOGY,
PITTSBURGH

During that summer, Andy worked with his brother Paul, selling fruits and vegetables from a truck. Andy sketched their customers, sometimes selling the pictures he drew. He also used his sketches to apply for a scholarship that helped him pay for the rest of his years at Carnegie.

Everyone at Carnegie agreed that Andy's art stood out. He certainly had his own style. His work always seemed to look perfect on the first try. He had a good eye for design, too. (Design means the way things are placed together in a work of art.) If another student asked for help, he suggested how to move images around in the picture to make it look better. His classmates thought he was a genius.

He also chose subjects that shocked people. For a city art exhibition, he submitted a drawing of a boy picking his nose. His picture was not chosen for the exhibit. However, it made people talk about him. Andy was learning how to get attention.

Andy hadn't decided what he would do after
college. At first, he thought he would be an art
teacher in Pittsburgh. Then he got a summer job
decorating the windows of a Pittsburgh department

store and discovered that he liked fashion and
design. One of his teachers thought Andy and
his friend Philip Pearlstein could be successful
as commercial artists, drawing pictures for

advertisements and magazines. So, after graduation, Andy and Philip left Pittsburgh for New York. They were ready to try to make it as artists in the big city.

Chapter 3
Ad Man

Andy and Philip moved into a small, drab apartment in the East Village of New York City. They visited the art directors at magazines and advertising agencies and showed their pictures from college. Art directors decide what kind of pictures go into magazine articles or the ads for different products. Andy's drawings were exactly the type of work that the art directors were looking for. He quickly got jobs from them.

There was plenty of work in the advertising and magazine business in the late 1940s and the 1950s. World War II was over, and soldiers came back from the war ready to return to work. They bought new cars and houses and furniture. Scientists who had been developing weapons for the war now created things that made life easier and more fun, like frozen dinners, modern stoves, and better refrigerators. Everyone seemed to be spending more money. Artists like Andy helped show them what to buy.

Andy was known for his "blotted line" drawings. Instead of even, flowing lines, his pictures were a mix of thin and thick lines, with dashes of empty space between them. His drawings were energetic and happy, as if the lines were jumping across the page. Art directors thought that it was the right style for the modern, cheerful 1950s, especially for fashion. Andy became famous for illustrating shoe ads for a company named I. Miller. His

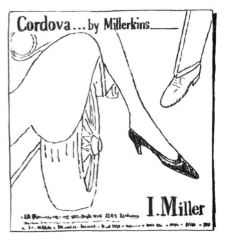

shoe drawings were splashed all over the huge ads the company placed in the Sunday newspapers.

By the early 1950s, Andy was known by everyone who worked in magazines or advertising. They knew him as Andy Warhol, though, not Andy Warhola. A few years earlier, a magazine he worked on mistakenly dropped the "a" and printed his name as just "Warhol." And Andy decided to keep it that way.

Andy's appearance changed as he made more money. He bought better clothes. He began seeing doctors to make his skin look better. But then, just when he was getting more comfortable with his physical appearance, he began to go bald.

At first, he wore a hat everywhere until friends persuaded him to try a wig. He wore wigs for the rest of his life.

Andy's mother, Julia, came to visit him in New York in 1952. His apartment was cold and messy.

He had a cat to help catch the many mice and rats. Julia decided to move to New York to cook and clean for Andy. Over time they got more and more cats. Julia named them all Sam.

Andy often had friends help with his illustrations. Now Julia helped, too. He would gather everyone together at his apartment or a café. They would each have a special task, like adding color to the drawings.

Julia wrote the words in her old-fashioned, curly
handwriting. Andy could work a lot more
quickly this way. He liked the idea of creating
an "art factory."

Andy had lots of friends, but not much luck in love. In the 1950s, gay people often felt it was safer to hide that they were gay. They weren't always treated kindly. Andy didn't care. He was sure enough of himself to be himself. However, he was shy about his looks. It was hard for him to compete with all the handsome people in New York's gay community. He dated a few men, then fell in love with a set designer, Charles Lisanby. They even went on an around-the-world trip together in 1956, but drifted apart after they returned. Andy did not have an easy time finding love.

By the mid-1950s, Andy had a lot to be proud of. The illustrations he drew for ads won awards from the Art Directors Club and the American Institute of Graphic Arts. He was making plenty of money. But something was missing. Andy dreamed of being an artist whose pictures were sold in art galleries and displayed in museums.

He wanted his name to be recognized by the whole world, not just by art directors in New York City.

Andy tried to get more people to see his drawings. He showed some of them in small art galleries. He worked with friends to create books of his drawings. He and Julia created a book of cat pictures called *25 Cats Name Sam and One Blue Pussy.* Andy published the books himself and sold them in gift shops. Everyone thought Andy's drawings were cute, but they still just thought of him as an advertising illustrator.

In a 1958 *Who's Who*–type book about people living and working in New York City, Andy's name wasn't listed under "Artists." It was listed under "Business."

Andy made a decision. He would still work in advertising, but he was going to spend more time trying to become a serious artist. In 1960, he bought a town house on Lexington Avenue with room for an art studio. His brothers came from Pittsburgh to help move Andy and Julia and all their cats and things to the new house. It was time for a big change.

Chapter 4
Breaking In

The art world was also changing. Since the 1940s, the most important paintings had been in a style called "Abstract Expressionism." They were made up of streaks, splatters, and blobs of paint, or big patches of color. These artists were "expressing" themselves through color and texture on the canvas.

By the late 1950s, some artists were breaking away from Abstract Expressionism. Jasper Johns painted pictures of familiar things like American flags, numbers, and bull's-eye targets. Robert Rauschenberg created works that combined painting, photographs, and actual objects like nails, rocks, and pieces of clothing.

IMPORTANT ABSTRACT EXPRESSIONISTS

JACKSON POLLOCK (1912-1956) WAS FAMOUS FOR PLACING A CANVAS ON THE FLOOR, THEN POURING AND DRIPPING PAINT ONTO IT. HE USED BRUSHES AND STICKS TO SWIRL THE PAINT, AND SOMETIMES MIXED SAND AND DIRT INTO THE PAINT TO CREATE BUMPS AND RIDGES. PEOPLE FELT HE MADE PAINTING A PHYSICAL ACTIVITY. SOME CALLED IT "ACTION PAINTING."

WILLEM DE KOONING (1904-1997) WAS KNOWN FOR A SERIES OF PAINTINGS OF WOMEN DONE IN ABSTRACT EXPRESSIONIST STYLE WITH LOTS OF BIG BRUSHSTROKES AND PAINT STREAKS.

HELEN FRANKENTHALER (1928-2011) WORKED LIKE JACKSON POLLOCK, WITH HER CANVAS ON THE FLOOR. SHE THINNED HER PAINT AND LET IT SOAK INTO THE CANVAS. HER PAINTINGS HAD A LIGHT, OPEN LOOK, LIKE WATERCOLORS. SHE WAS A LEADER OF THE "COLOR FIELD" BRANCH OF ABSTRACT EXPRESSIONISM.

MARK ROTHKO (1903-1970) WAS ALSO A COLOR FIELD PAINTER, WITH WORKS MADE UP OF LARGE BLOCKS OF STRONG COLORS. HE SAID HIS PAINTINGS EXPRESSED "BASIC HUMAN EMOTIONS."

Andy had no interest in expressing himself through streaks of color and blobs of paint. Painting real, everyday things—like in the artwork by Rauschenberg and Johns—made more sense to him. But he didn't want to copy other artists. He wanted to do something new and different.

He painted the front pages of newspapers,

Coke bottles, and comic-strip characters like Superman and Popeye. But Andy worried that people might not think these kinds of paintings were important works of art. Although a department store put his comic-book paintings in their window display, he couldn't find an art gallery to give him his own show.

One day, Andy and a friend went to the famous Leo Castelli Gallery to look at paintings. Andy desperately wanted to have a show there. Ivan Karp, the associate director of the gallery, showed them some new pictures by an artist named Roy Lichtenstein. They were all based on comic-book illustrations. They didn't have any of the "artistic" touches Andy had put on his pictures, though.

They were painted with bold, clean lines. They looked exactly like the drawings in a real comic book. Andy's heart sank. He and Lichtenstein were painting the same type of thing! But Lichtenstein was doing it better. No one would care about Andy's comic-book paintings now.

Andy always liked to talk about what he was painting and what he should paint. In November 1961, Andy invited his friend Muriel Latow to his house. She owned a small art gallery, and Andy thought she always had good ideas.

"Just tell me what to paint," Andy said.

"That'll cost you fifty dollars," Muriel said.

Andy didn't really want to pay Muriel, but was anxious for new ideas. He wrote her a check for fifty dollars.

Muriel's idea was for Andy to paint something people see every day, like a can of soup. How about really big paintings of Campbell's soup cans?

Andy loved the idea. Everyone knew what the red-and-white Campbell's soup label looked like. His own mother often made him Campbell's soup for lunch.

But he knew he couldn't paint the soup cans in his old comic-book style. In early 1962, Andy asked his friend Emile de Antonio to look at some paintings. He showed "De" two pictures of Coke bottles. One had paint drips and sketchy lines like the Abstract Expressionists used. The other was just a simple painting of the bottle, done with smooth, clear lines. De immediately told him to forget the drips and blobs. The clean painting was bold and modern. Andy agreed. This was his new style.

Andy went to work painting his soup cans.

Each painting was a different flavor of soup. He didn't even try to make them look realistic. Instead, it looked like he was painting an illustration of a soup can label!

In December, Irving Blum, an art dealer from California, came to New York. He had met Andy before but hadn't really liked any of his work.

He liked the soup cans, though. He asked Andy to show them at the Ferus Gallery in Los Angeles in the summer of 1962. Andy was delighted.

Chapter 5
Pop Art

People were beginning to talk about Johns
and Rauschenberg. Some called them the "New
Realists" because they painted real things. A
May 1962 article in *Time* magazine called it the
"Slice-of-Cake School" of art, because of artist

Wayne Thiebaud's
paintings of ordinary
food, like cake. The
article included a
picture of Andy
standing in front
of one of his soup
can paintings,
pretending to eat
out of a can of soup.

By the end of the year, people were calling the new art "Pop Art," which was short for "popular art." Pop Art wasn't about feelings and big ideas. It was about the things people saw in stores or on billboards or in fast-food restaurants. And Andy loved all those things.

Andy thought that it was okay to celebrate everyday life. He didn't think that culture and art only had to be about serious and important things. It could also be about common, fun, inexpensive things. He said that he painted what he liked. And Andy liked painting things that shocked people.

In 1962, Andy made a big change in the way he painted by using the silk-screen process. Silk screening begins by cutting an image into a stencil, then attaching it to a mesh screen. The screen is placed over a piece of paper or fabric. When ink is pushed across the screen with a squeegee, the ink leaves a print of the image.

With silk screening, Andy could cover a canvas with rows of the same printed image by using the same stencil over and over. Andy loved the process because it looked like the pictures were printed by a machine. But he still could change how each picture looked by using different colors or making the image blurry. He filled canvases with pictures of the rock star Elvis Presley and the movie star Marilyn Monroe.

For the Marilyn pictures, Andy painted a slash of red on the canvas where her lips would be printed, and blue where she would have blue eye shadow. He painted an outline of yellow for her hair. Sometimes when he printed, the stencil didn't line up exactly with the colors. The lip color might be partly on her cheek and the eye shadow would be next to her eyelids, not on them. Andy believed that mistakes—and images that looked less than perfect—could be interesting.

People began to know Andy's name after the *Time* magazine article and Ferus Gallery show.

He sold some paintings. But he still hadn't had a New York show. He worried that he would fall behind the other Pop Art artists.

But then Eleanor Ward offered Andy his own show at the Stable Gallery. He also had been asked to take part in a group show with several other artists, called *The International Exhibition of New Realists*, at the Sidney Janis Gallery, also in New York City. The Janis Gallery was the first established New York City gallery to show Pop Art.

The New Realists show was a huge success.
Newspapers and magazines wrote about it. Andy's
show at the Stable opened only a week later and
drew big crowds that included many young people.

They weren't usually part of the wealthy, older art gallery crowd. But they were interested in Pop Art.

Andy had to wait longer than the other Pop artists to get his own show, but that turned out to be a good thing. By the time his show opened, people knew about Pop Art. They wanted to see it. Every painting in the show at the Stable sold. Andy was a success.

Chapter 6
Factory Life

Andy had one assistant who helped him with advertising projects, and a new assistant, Gerard Malanga, who had silk-screening experience. With his assistants and Julia, Andy's town house was becoming crowded. In late 1963, he found a new studio space to rent in a building on East 47th Street that used to be a hat factory.

Andy moved his studio there in January 1964. He asked his friend Billy Linich (who later became known as "Billy Name") to cover the walls in silver paint and aluminum foil. He thought silver was a very modern color. It reminded him of the suits worn by astronauts. It took Billy almost three months to cover the entire space in silver. He spent so much time working there that he moved into a small corner of the studio and lived there for the rest of the decade.

Billy was a lighting designer who lived in New York's East Village. Andy loved to go out, and Gerard knew how to find all kinds of interesting people and events in the busy East Village art scene. The East Village was different from the Upper East Side, where all the important art galleries were and where wealthy art buyers lived. The East Village was filled

GERARD MALANGA

with old buildings that weren't in very good shape. Struggling artists could afford to live there.

Andy and Gerard went to modern dance shows,

poetry readings in cafés, and rock concerts. Andy was especially fascinated by the "underground filmmakers," who showed their short, experimental films on the walls of people's apartments.

Andy used to wear button-down shirts and ties like all the other people who worked in advertising. Now he had a new look. It was more relaxed: black jeans, a black leather jacket, and boots. His wigs were more silver than white. He often wore sunglasses. Andy was still shy. But now when he was quiet, people thought he was being mysterious.

Andy and Gerard were working on Andy's next show for the Stable. They silk-screened labels of products like Brillo pads onto giant boxes. They stacked them around the gallery. It looked like a grocery store. Many people came to see them, but few boxes were sold. Even big fans of Pop Art didn't want to have piles of pot-scrubber boxes in their living rooms!

The party Andy threw after the show opened was a bigger success than the actual show. His uptown art buyer friends and his downtown artist friends all came together in the silver-covered studio.

People who lived in fancy apartments on Park Avenue didn't usually attend parties with shabby poets and dancers. But that was changing, especially at the Factory, which is what everyone now called Andy's silver studio.

POP-TART/POP ART?

IN 1963, POST CEREALS ANNOUNCED THAT
THEY WERE GOING TO MAKE NEW BREAKFAST

PASTRY SQUARES FILLED
WITH A SWEET JAM-
LIKE FILLING.
POST CALLED
THEM "COUNTRY
SQUARES." THE
NEW PRODUCT
COULD BE
HEATED IN
A TOASTER.
BUT POST
WAS STILL DEVELOPING IT. IT WOULDN'T BE IN
STORES FOR ANOTHER SIX MONTHS.

THAT WAS ENOUGH TIME FOR ANOTHER BIG
FOOD COMPANY, KELLOGG'S, TO MAKE THEIR OWN
VERSION. THEY NEEDED A GOOD NAME. ANDY
WARHOL AND POP ART WERE ALL OVER THE
NEWS. AND BECAUSE THE PASTRY WAS MADE
FROM DOUGH SIMILAR TO WHAT WAS USED FOR
PIES OR TARTS, KELLOGG'S THOUGHT THE NAME
"POP-TART" WOULD BE A FUN PLAY ON POP ART.

KELLOGG'S RUSHED FOUR FLAVORS OF
POP-TARTS INTO GROCERY STORES. THE FIRST

SHIPMENTS SOLD OUT IMMEDIATELY. POP-TARTS WERE A BIG HIT.

WHEN POST FINALLY GOT THEIR COUNTRY SQUARES INTO STORES, THEY FLOPPED. SOME PEOPLE BLAMED THE NAME. "COUNTRY" SOUNDED OLD-FASHIONED, AND "SQUARE" WAS 1960S SLANG FOR BORING. "POP-TART" SOUNDED COOL AND MODERN.

MILLIONS OF POP-TARTS, IN TWENTY-NINE FLAVORS, ARE STILL SOLD TODAY.

At first, people called it the Factory because it actually used to be a hat factory. Later, people said it was because Andy produced art like a factory. He was even quoted in a magazine, saying, "I'm becoming a factory." But Andy never referred to his work space as the Factory. He always called it the "studio."

Soon, all kinds of people began to show up at the Factory. An elevator opened right into the studio. Anyone could walk in. Some of Andy's friends hung out there all day. Other people came to see Andy about art. Some just came because they thought it was a cool place to be seen.

Andy kept creating more artwork. He now showed at the Castelli Gallery—the same gallery that once turned him down because his work looked too much like Roy Lichtenstein's paintings. Andy was now famous for his own style. Andy was not just any Pop artist. Many people thought he was *the* Pop artist.

In 1965, Andy and some friends flew to Paris, where an important gallery was showing some of his work. Andy made a big announcement there. He was retiring from painting. He was going to make movies.

Chapter 7
Making Movies

Andy had actually started making movies
in 1963. His first movie was called *Sleep*.

In *Sleep*, Andy filmed one of his friends sleeping—
for over five hours!

All of Andy's early movies showed people
doing ordinary things. One was of Billy giving
someone a haircut. In another, Andy filmed
artist Robert Indiana eating a mushroom. In
Empire, Andy set up his camera to face the
Empire State Building. For eight hours, the only
action in the film is when the building's lights
are turned off. The movie continues for hours
with nothing but the dark night sky on the
screen.

Many people thought Andy's movies were
boring. He *also* thought they were boring, but
boring in a good way. He said they showed what
you would see if you looked out a window or sat
on a park bench and watched people. Just like
he thought soup cans could be art, he thought
everyday events could be movies.

Andy thought he could create movie stars just

as well as anyone in Hollywood. He didn't want people to act for him, though. He thought the right kind of people would shine on-screen just by being themselves. Andy called his actors his "superstars."

Some were his friends from the East Village. Others had heard about the Factory and came

EDIE SEDGWICK

there hoping that Andy would make them famous.

Edie Sedgwick was one of the most famous Factory "superstars." She was young. She was beautiful. She was wild. She came from a rich family in California and left college to come to New York to be a model. She wanted to be an actress, but she couldn't act. That was okay with Andy. The people in his movies didn't need to act. He just wanted them to look good and be themselves. Edie looked very good on-screen.

Andy and Edie went everywhere together. She dyed her hair to match Andy's silver wigs.

Newspapers and magazines called her the "Girl of the Year." Someone asked Andy who should play him in a movie. He said Edie. Although it never happened, Andy was probably not joking. Sadly, Edie died in 1971 from a drug overdose. She was only twenty-eight.

Andy made dozens of movies throughout the 1960s. Even though he claimed he had retired from painting, he still created many silk-screen portraits. He also continued to work in advertising if the assignment interested him. Andy worked hard all day, and then he and his friends went out to parties at night.

Andy took diet pills to stay thin. But they also kept him awake for hours. So he took even more pills to help him sleep. At the

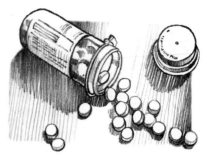

time, it was very easy for Andy and many other people to get prescriptions from their doctors. Other people at the Factory took illegal drugs to make them feel good. They thought drugs helped them be more creative and more energetic. But the drugs were also very addictive and dangerous. Eventually, drug use ruined the lives of some of Andy's closest friends in addition to Edie's.

In 1965, an art museum in Philadelphia planned a big show of Andy's paintings. They announced that Andy and some of his superstars were coming from New York for the opening. The museum was so crowded that night, museum security took the paintings down from the walls because they were worried they might get damaged. When Andy, Edie, and others from the Factory arrived, the crowd went wild. They pushed forward to get close to Andy. It was more like a rock concert than an art show. When Andy and his friends became trapped on a staircase, someone cut a hole in the ceiling to get them out.

It was scary, but Andy loved it. He had always wanted to be famous like the movie stars he worshipped when he was a boy. Now he was being treated like a star himself.

Chapter 8
The Exploding Plastic Inevitable

In 1966, Andy thought that managing a rock band would be a good way to make some extra money. With the help of Gerard and a young filmmaker named Paul Morrissey, he found a band called the Velvet Underground, led by a guitarist, singer, and songwriter named Lou Reed. Andy decided he would become their manager.

PAUL MORRISSEY AND LOU REED

Andy and Paul hoped they had found the next Beatles. But the Velvet Underground was the opposite of the popular British band. The Velvet Underground's music was strange and difficult. The lyrics to their songs were about drugs and subjects not mentioned in *other* popular rock songs.

The band seemed perfect for the kind of show Andy wanted to put on, though. He asked them to add a female singer, a German model named Nico. She didn't sing that well, but she looked good. They rented a hall in the East Village and called the show Andy Warhol's *Exploding Plastic Inevitable*.

NICO

The show opened in April 1966. The Velvets played their music while Factory superstars danced onstage with them.

Movies played on the walls and on the band itself. Lights flashed all over the hall. The show was noisy and wild. Some people loved it. Others hated it. But by now, Andy was used to that sort of reaction to his work.

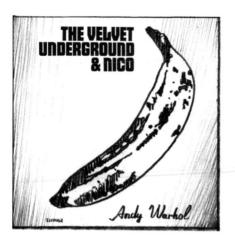

Andy helped pay for the Velvet Underground to record an album. He designed an album cover with a banana sticker that could be peeled off. But the sticker was hard to produce. The record company used a drawing of the banana instead. The album didn't sell well. The Velvet Underground didn't have any hit songs. They soon stopped working with Andy. Though a failure when it was released, the record *The Velvet Underground & Nico* has become one of the most influential rock albums in history. And although Andy gave up his dream of managing a band, he continued to host many important rock stars at the Factory, including Jim Morrison of the Doors and Mick Jagger of the Rolling Stones.

In 1966, Andy finally made a hit movie. *The Chelsea Girls* was filmed in New York at the Chelsea Hotel, where some of the Factory superstars lived. *The Chelsea Girls* didn't tell one story. It just showed the superstars talking and

making up their own stories. Andy filmed so many scenes that he decided to show two scenes side by side at the same time on movie screens. Some scenes were funny while others were sad. *The Chelsea Girls* played in theaters all over the United States.

At the end of 1967, the owners of the Factory's East 47th Street building decided to tear it down, so Andy needed to find a new location for the Factory. Paul Morrissey picked out a studio in a building in Union Square.

JED JOHNSON

While they were fixing it up, they hired a young man named Jed Johnson. He started out sweeping floors, but later helped direct several films. He and Andy began to date.

The new Factory was bright and airy with white walls. It looked more like a modern office. But the Factory was still a very casual place. Anyone could come to the Factory.

A woman named Valerie Solanas had played a small role in one of Andy's movies, but she really wanted to be a writer. She asked Andy to produce a play she wrote, but he wasn't interested. On June 3, 1968, she came to the Factory looking for Andy. She waited outside until Andy arrived with a few other people. They rode up in the elevator together and went into the studio. The phone rang. It was a call for Andy. He was on the phone when Valerie approached him. She took out a gun and shot several times. A bullet entered the left side of Andy's body and pierced several organs. Valerie then shot a visiting art critic in the hip. She left in the elevator and someone called an ambulance. Gerard Malanga

arrived and saw what had happened. He rushed uptown to tell Andy's mother, Julia, before she saw and heard the news on television.

Doctors operated on Andy for hours. They weren't sure if he would live, but he survived. Andy had to stay in the hospital for almost two months.

Jed moved into Andy's house to take care of him and Julia. Andy was in pain from his injuries for the rest of his life.

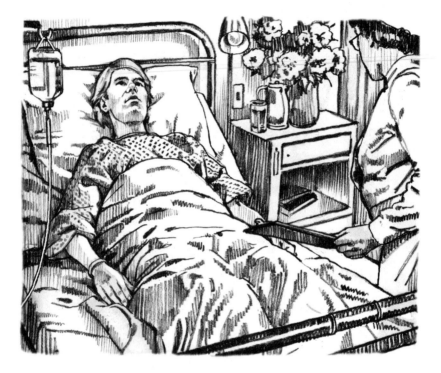

Valerie Solanas turned herself in to the police and was sent to prison for three years. No one ever really understood why she shot Andy.

Chapter 9
Superstar

Andy was frightened by the shooting. He was scared to go to the Factory alone. Security became a big concern for him. People were no longer allowed to come there just to hang out. Anyone using illegal drugs was asked to stay away. The Factory was now much more of a business.

Rich and famous people wanted Warhol portraits of themselves. The demand on Andy's time made the prices of the paintings rise higher and higher.

In 1969, Andy started a magazine called *Interview*.

It was a magazine about movie stars, rock stars, models, and fashion designers, or anyone else who was cool or important at the moment.

These were the people Andy spent most of his time with now. In the early 1960s, he had done portraits of movie stars he admired from a distance. Now he was friends with them.

Andy's mother had returned to Pittsburgh in 1970, and died there two years later. After Julia's death, Andy's personal life opened up. After living with his mother for nearly twenty years, he was free to socialize and to travel. He seemed to be someplace different every night, whether in New York or another city or another country. He went to openings of art shows, openings of plays, openings of movies. Most often, he could be found at a nightclub called Studio 54.

Everyone who was anyone went to Studio 54. Rock stars, movie stars, athletes, models,

and millionaires from Europe and Asia flew to
New York just to go to Studio 54. Andy loved
being surrounded by the famous and wealthy
people there. But now he was famous and wealthy,
too. People came to the club to be seen with
Andy Warhol.

Andy always brought his camera to Studio 54.
Andy thought photographs were like a diary.

STUDIO 54

IN 1977, STEVE RUBELL, A RESTAURANT OWNER, AND IAN SCHRAGER, A LAWYER, BOUGHT AN OLD THEATER AT 254 WEST 54TH STREET IN NEW YORK CITY. THEY TURNED IT INTO ONE OF THE BEST-KNOWN NIGHTCLUBS IN HISTORY. RUBELL AND SCHRAGER PUT UP A VELVET ROPE IN FRONT OF THE DOOR, AND A DOORMAN DECIDED WHO GOT IN.

IAN SCHRAGER AND STEVE RUBELL

THE WEALTHY AND FAMOUS WALKED RIGHT INTO THE CLUB. THEN THE DOORMAN PICKED OUT THE MOST BEAUTIFUL OR INTERESTING PEOPLE WAITING IN THE LONG LINES AND LET THEM IN. RUBELL SAID, "WE WANT EVERYONE TO BE FUN AND GOOD-LOOKING." THE CLUB WAS KNOWN FOR ITS THEATRICAL SETS AND FLASHING LIGHTS. IT WAS ALWAYS PACKED WITH PEOPLE DANCING TO LOUD DISCO MUSIC. RUBELL AND SCHRAGER'S FINAL PARTY AT STUDIO 54 WAS ON FEBRUARY 4, 1980.

Andy used photographs to keep a record of where he was and whom he was with. He loved to take pictures of all the well-dressed people having fun at the club. He was still thrilled by celebrities, even though he was now one himself. Andy said everyone loved to see stars.

Jed found a new town house for Andy, and in 1974 they moved into 57 East 66th Street.

Jed decorated the entire house. Jed and Andy shared two dachshunds, named Archie and Amos, whom they loved very much. When Jed left Andy in 1980 to start a business as an interior designer, he and Andy shared custody of the dogs.

In 1983, Andy began to work with a young artist named Jean-Michel Basquiat, who had started as a graffiti artist, spray-painting pictures onto the walls of buildings. Young artists like Basquiat admired how Andy had found a way to earn money with

JEAN-MICHEL BASQUIAT

his art and make himself a celebrity. Andy helped Jean-Michel by bringing him to parties and introducing him to the wealthy people he knew.

They also painted together. Andy painted famous labels and products while Basquiat added figures in his graffiti-like style.

Andy made money easily now. He created art for advertising again. He appeared in commercials and showed up in movies. He was in an episode of the television show *The Love Boat* and appeared on *Saturday Night Live*.

Andy would often go to a party, not speak much while he was there, then go home and call friends and talk all night about what he had seen and heard. Sometimes he called friends and they'd watch the same TV shows,

and sometimes he'd call a friend and they'd eat breakfast together while on the phone. One woman who worked at *Interview* said she thought he was more interested in hearing stories about *her* dates than in having any of his own! Andy always taped his phone conversations. He published several books based on the tapes: *a: a novel* (1968), *The Philosophy of Andy Warhol (From A to B and Back Again)* (1977), and *POPism: The Warhol '60s* (1980).

But Andy did keep one thing private: his deep religious faith. Few people knew that he attended mass every Sunday and often stopped into church during the week as well. He wore a cross around his neck and kept a prayer book by his bed. He even volunteered at a church homeless shelter.

In 1985, the Campbell Soup Company asked Andy to design the labels for a line of dry soup mixes. What a long way he had come since 1962, when everyone knew Campbell's Soup, but not Andy Warhol. By the time he was in his mid-fifties, people looked at Campbell's Soup labels and thought of Andy Warhol.

ANDY WARHOL IN HIS OWN WORDS

"I LIKE BORING THINGS."

"POP ART IS FOR EVERYONE."

"AN ARTIST IS SOMEBODY WHO PRODUCES THINGS THAT PEOPLE DON'T NEED TO HAVE."

"THEY ALWAYS SAY TIME CHANGES THINGS, BUT YOU ACTUALLY HAVE TO CHANGE THEM YOURSELF."

"I THINK HAVING LAND AND NOT RUINING IT IS THE MOST BEAUTIFUL ART THAT ANYBODY COULD EVER WANT TO OWN."

"ART IS WHAT YOU CAN GET AWAY WITH."

"SOMETIMES THE LITTLE TIMES YOU DON'T THINK ARE ANYTHING WHILE THEY'RE HAPPENING TURN OUT TO BE WHAT MARKS A WHOLE PERIOD OF YOUR LIFE."

Chapter 10
Legacy

Andy began to have stomach pains in the winter of 1987. He had never liked going to the doctor. But his friends finally persuaded him to do something about the pain. The doctor told Andy that his gallbladder was infected and that he would need surgery. Andy didn't like that idea, but he had no other choice. He had the operation

on February 21, 1987. Everything seemed to go well. But overnight his health worsened. Andy died suddenly on the morning of February 22, at age fifty-eight.

Andy was buried in Pittsburgh near his mother and father. A few months later, there was a memorial service for him in St. Patrick's

Cathedral in New York City. More than two thousand people attended. Andy had made many, many friends during his short life.

Andy died an extremely wealthy man. His town house was filled with art, antiques, furniture, sculptures, and jewelry. There were cookie jars, toys, and knickknacks. Drawers were filled with jewels. Everything Andy owned was sold at an auction for a total of about $25 million.

Andy had arranged for most of his money to be used to start the Andy Warhol Museum and the Andy Warhol Foundation for the Visual Arts in Pittsburgh, which teaches people about Andy's life and work. The foundation also gives money to support young artists and arts groups.

Andy did an amazing amount of work in his lifetime. He created about thirty-two thousand paintings and prints, and many films.

His paintings are now very valuable. In 2008, his *Eight Elvises* (1963), sold for $100 million!

ANDY'S INFLUENCE

THE INFLUENCE OF ANDY WARHOL CAN BE SEEN IN MANY LATE TWENTIETH-CENTURY ARTISTS WHO TRY TO MATCH ANDY'S ABILITY TO TURN HIMSELF INTO A CELEBRITY AND A "BRAND" THAT CAN BE SOLD. BRITISH ARTIST DAMIEN HIRST HAS OWNED RESTAURANTS AND SHOPS. JAPANESE ARTIST TAKASHI MURAKAMI HAS GIFT STORES THAT TRAVEL WITH HIS EXHIBITS, AND DESIGNS EVERYTHING FROM HANDBAGS TO TOYS. IT'S NOW COMMON FOR ARTISTS TO BE SEEN AT CELEBRITY EVENTS AND HAVE GALLERY OPENINGS THAT ARE MORE LIKE PARTIES THAN ART SHOWS.

Andy showed that everyday things can be art. His portrait style, with repeated printed images, is copied everywhere. Street vendors sell pictures of today's celebrities done in the style of his Marilyn Monroe silk-screened portraits. Websites can turn an ordinary photo into a "Warhol-style" portrait.

Andy believed people could be superstars just by being themselves. Now people do that every day through social media, on YouTube, and on reality TV.

In 2012, Campbell's Soup celebrated the fiftieth anniversary of the Ferus Gallery show with a set of limited edition, Warhol-inspired soup can labels. Soup cans had become the art Andy always knew they were. Andy would have liked that.

TIMELINE OF
ANDY WARHOL'S LIFE

1928 — Born Andrew Warhola on August 6 in Pittsburgh to Julia and Andrej Warhola

1936–1937 — Begins free art classes at Carnegie Museum; has rheumatic fever

1945 — Enrolls in the Department of Painting and Design at the Carnegie Institute of Technology (now Carnegie Mellon University)

1949 — Graduates from Carnegie Institute of Technology; moves to New York and begins career as commercial artist

1956 — Has shoe ad drawing included in the Museum of Modern Art's show *Recent Drawings, U.S.A.*

1960 — Moves into town house at 1342 Lexington Avenue to have more room to do serious artwork

1962 — Has soup can paintings exhibited in Ferus Gallery in Los Angeles; begins paintings of celebrities like Marilyn Monroe; starts to use silk-screen technique

1964 — Moves studio into East 47th Street building that becomes known as "The Factory;" has "Brillo box" exhibition at the Stable Gallery

1966 — Begins working with the Velvet Underground and features them in touring multimedia shows *Andy Warhol's Up-Tight* and *Exploding Plastic Inevitable*; *The Chelsea Girls*, his most successful movie, opens

1968 — The Factory moves to Union Square; Andy is shot by Valerie Solanas and barely survives

1969 — First issue of *Interview* magazine appears

1980 — Publishes *POPism: The Warhol '60s*

1983 — Collaborates on paintings with Jean-Michel Basquiat

1985 — Appears on TV shows *The Love Boat* and *Saturday Night Live*

1987 — Dies on February 22 after gallbladder surgery

TIMELINE OF
THE WORLD

Campbell's Soup introduces its red-and-white label	1898
Marilyn Monroe is born	1926
The stock market crashes and the Great Depression begins	1929
Ruth Wakefield invents the chocolate-chip cookie	1930
Pearl Harbor is bombed; the United States enters World War II	1941
Jackie Robinson becomes the first African American to play major-league baseball	1947
The first restaurant in the McDonald's chain opens	1954
President Kennedy is assassinated	1963
The Beatles come to America	1964
Star Trek premieres	1966
Neil Armstrong becomes the first man to walk on the moon	1969
The first e-mail is sent	1971
Steve Jobs and Steve Wozniak introduce the Apple I computer	1976
Star Wars is released	1977
The video game *Pac-Man* is introduced	1980
MTV begins	1981
The Simpsons premieres	1989

BIBLIOGRAPHY

Angelotti, Martina, Valentina Ciuffi, and Veronica Lenza. **Pop Art**. Vercelli, Italy: White Star Publishers, 2011.

Bourdon, David. **Warhol**. New York: Harry N. Abrams, Inc., 1989.

Goldsmith, Kenneth, ed. **I'll Be Your Mirror: The Selected Andy Warhol Interviews, 1962–1987**. New York: Carroll & Graf Publishers, 2004.

Indiana, Gary. **Andy Warhol and the Can That Sold the World**. New York: Basic Books, 2010.

Scherman, Tony, and David Dalton. **Pop: The Genius of Andy Warhol**. New York: HarperCollins, 2009.

Warhol, Andy, and Pat Hackett. **POPism: The Warhol '60s**. New York: Harcourt Brace Jovanovich, 1980.

WEBSITES

Gompertz, Will. "Andy Warhol's Great Secret." Salon.com. http://www.salon.com/2012/10/21/andy_warhols_great_secret/.

McGill, Douglas C. "Andy Warhol, Pop Artist, Dies." *The New York Times*. February 23, 1987. http://www.nytimes.com/1987/02/23/obituaries/andy-warhol-pop-artist-dies.html?pagewanted=all&src=pm.

"Modern Art Timeline 2" (1916–1975). Arty Factory. http://www.artyfactory.com/art_appreciation/timelines/modern_art_timeline_part_2.html.

"Modern Art—Visual Arts Movements: 1880–1970." About.com—Art History. http://arthistory.about.com/library/outlines/blmodern.htm.

O'Brien, Glenn. "Andy Warhol's Influence on Art Today." Departures. http://www.departures.com/articles/andy-warhols-influence-on-art-today.

Swenson, G. R. "What Is Pop Art?" November 1963. Art News. http://www.artnews.com/2007/11/01/top-ten-artnews-stories-the-first-word-on-pop.